The COVID-19 lockdown is killing more people than it is saving

By Daniel Alman

Table of Contents

About the author

Since there are quite a few people named Daniel Alman in the world, it is worth noting that this particular Daniel Alman was born in 1971, and has spent his entire life so far living in the Squirrel Hill neighborhood of Pittsburgh, Pennsylvania. He has a bachelor's degree in mathematics from the University of Pittsburgh, but even more importantly (at least in his opinion), he attended the Montessori Centre Academy in Glenshaw, Pennsylvania, for ten years, beginning at the age of two. His blog is at

https://danfromsquirrelhill.wordpress.com/

Date of Publication

This book was published on March 27, 2021.

Fair Use

All quotes and excerpts used in this book are attributed under fair use policy.

The COVID-19 lockdown is killing more people than it is saving

The COVID-19 lockdown is killing more people than it is saving.

These are the CDC's estimated survival rates, by age, for people who contract COVID-19:

https://web.archive.org/web/2020092318 5857/https://www.cdc.gov/coronavirus/2 019-ncov/hcp/planning-scenarios.html

0 to 19: 99.997%

20 to 49: 99.98%

50 to 69: 99.5%

70+: 94.6%

For most age groups, the survival rate is quite high. In my opinion, this does not justify a lockdown of the general population.

Now let's take a look at my many reasons for thinking that the lockdown is killing more people than it is saving:

This study claims that the lockdown is destroying 10 times as many Quality Adjusted Life Years as it is saving:

https://macdonaldlaurier.ca/files/pdf/20201209_Rethinking_lockdowns_Joffe_COMMENTARY_FWeb.pdf

The National Cancer Institute estimates that there could be 10,000 additional breast and colorectal deaths over the next decade as a result of missed screenings and delayed diagnoses.

Source:
https://www.wjhg.com/2020/09/08/cancer-screenings-down-nationwide-during-the-covid-19-pandemic/

Cancer surgeries and organ transplants are being put off for coronavirus.

Source:
https://www.cnbc.com/2020/04/08/op-ed-cancer-surgeries-and-organ-transplants-are-being-put-off-for-coronavirus.html

Higher rates of unemployment correlate very strongly with higher rates of suicide and drug overdoses.

Source:
https://thefederalist.com/2020/03/30/how-shutting-down-the-economy-much-longer-could-kill-tens-of-thousands-of-americans/

A report by the United Nations cites the predicted harm that will happen to tens of millions of children in low income countries as a result of the COVID-19 global wide shutdown.

Examples of this harm to children include increases in malnutrition, loss of education, increased rates of teen pregnancy, reduced access to health care, reduced rates of vaccination, increased rates of infectious disease, increased rates of water borne illness, and increased rates of death.

Source:
https://unsdg.un.org/sites/default/files/2020-04/160420_Covid_Children_Policy_Brief.pdf

Anxiety from reactions to Covid-19 will destroy at least seven times more years of life than can be saved by lockdowns.

Source:
https://www.justfacts.com/news_covid-19_anxiety_lockdowns_life_destroyed_saved

The Hill wrote:

"Childhood vaccine rates for preventable diseases like measles and whooping cough have fallen during the COVID-19 pandemic, raising the possibility of an additional health crisis."

"In New York City… the number of vaccine doses administered from March 23 to May 9 fell 63 percent compared with the same period last year."

"In children older than 2 years, it fell 91 percent…"

"… Doctors offices have been closed…"

"… The numbers in New York match a

national trend…"

"… from mid-March to mid-April, doctors in the federally funded Vaccines for Children program for the uninsured ordered about 2.5 million fewer doses of all routine non-influenza vaccines and 250,000 fewer doses of measles-containing vaccines compared to the same period in 2019…"

Source:
https://thehill.com/policy/healthcare/498797-childhood-vaccine-rates-plummet-amid-coronavirus-pandemic-risking-new

The New York Times wrote:

"Polio and measles could surge after disruption of vaccine programs. A new study of 129 countries found that the interruption of inoculation efforts could put 80 million babies at risk of getting deadly, preventable diseases."

Source:
https://www.nytimes.com/2020/05/22/health/coronavirus-polio-measles-immunizations.html

This BBC article is called, "Why most Covid-19 deaths won't be from the virus."

https://www.bbc.com/future/article/20200528-why-most-covid-19-deaths-wont-be-from-the-virus

The global lockdown was put into place based on the bogus, false, and extremely inaccurate Imperial College model.

Sweden did not have a lockdown.

Experts, who cited the Imperial College model, predicted that Sweden would have 40,000 COVID-19 deaths by May 1, 2020.

The actual number was 2,769.

The same bogus Imperial College model was used to implement the lockdowns for the rest of the world.

Sources:
https://www.telegraph.co.uk/news/2020/05/05/sweden-suppressed-infection-rates-without-lockdown/

https://www.aier.org/article/imperial-college-model-applied-to-sweden-yields-preposterous-results/

Nobel Prize-winning scientist Michael Levitt said, "the damage done by lockdown will exceed any saving of lives by a huge factor"

Source is on the next page.

https://www.theblaze.com/news/nobel-prize-winning-scientist-shares-covid-19-data-showing-strict-lockdowns-were-an-overreaction

This next link is to is a scientific paper called "Full lockdown policies in Western Europe countries have no evident impacts on the COVID-19 epidemic."

https://www.medrxiv.org/content/10.1101/2020.04.24.20078717v1.full.pdf

Do lockdowns save many lives? In most places, the data say no.

Source:
https://www.wsj.com/articles/do-lockdowns-save-many-lives-is-most-places-the-data-say-no-11587930911?mod=opinion_lead_pos5

U.S. medical testing, cancer screenings plunge during coronavirus outbreak – data firm analysis

Source: https://www.reuters.com/article/us-health-coronavirus-usa-screenings-exc/exclusive-u-s-medical-testing-cancer-screenings-plunge-during-coronavirus-outbreak-data-firm-analysis-idUSKCN22A0DY

Some medical experts fear more people are dying from untreated emergencies than from the coronavirus.

Source: https://www.nytimes.com/2020/04/25/health/coronavirus-heart-stroke.html

How the COVID-19 lockdown will take its own toll on health

Source is on the next page.

https://www.reuters.com/article/us-health-coronavirus-usa-cost-special-r/special-report-how-the-covid-19-lockdown-will-take-its-own-toll-on-health-idUSKBN21L20C

A study of hospitalized COVID-19 patients in New York showed that 66% of them were people who stayed home

Source: https://www.forbes.com/sites/lisettevoytko/2020/05/06/majority-of-new-coronavirus-cases-in-new-york-are-from-people-staying-at-home-not-traveling-or-working

End all restrictions, they were unnecessary, Hebrew University researchers say

Source is on the next page.

https://www.timesofisrael.com/end-all-restrictions-they-were-unnecessary-hebrew-university-researchers-say/

A scientific paper states:

"Background: The pandemic caused by COVID-19 has forced governments to implement strict social mitigation strategies to reduce the morbidity and mortality from acute infections. These strategies however carry a significant risk for mental health which can lead to increased short-term and long-term mortality and is currently not included in modelling the impact of the pandemic. Methods: We used years of life lost (YLL) as the main outcome measure as applied to Switzerland as an exemplar. We focused on suicide, depression, alcohol use disorder, childhood trauma due to domestic violence, changes in marital status and social isolation as these are known to increase YLL in the context of imposed restriction in social contact and freedom of movement. We stipulated a minimum duration of mitigation of 3 months based on current public health plans. Results: The study projects that the average person would suffer 0.205 YLL due to psychosocial consequence of COVID-19 mitigation measures. However, this loss would be entirely borne by 2.1% of the population, who will suffer an average 9.79 YLL. Conclusions: The results presented here are likely to underestimate the true impact of the mitigation strategies on YLL. However, they highlight the need for public health models to expand their scope in order to provide better estimates of the risks and benefits of mitigation."

Source:
https://www.medrxiv.org/content/10.1101/2020.04.17.20069716v3

In the U.S., the lockdown caused 1.4 million health care workers to be laid off:

Source: https://thehill.com/policy/healthcare/496816-health-care-industry-decimated-by-coronavirus-loses-14-million-jobs

The Atlantic wrote:

"Take the Shutdown Skeptics Seriously"

"Americans should carefully consider the potential costs of prolonged shutdowns lest they cause more deaths or harm to the vulnerable than they spare…"

"… minimizing the number of COVID-19 deaths today or a month from now or six months from now may or may not minimize the human costs of the pandemic when the full spectrum of human consequences is considered…"

"… the warnings of thoughtful shutdown skeptics warrant careful study…"

Source: https://www.theatlantic.com/ideas/archive/2020/05/take-shutdown-skeptics-seriously/611419/

Cyril H. Wecht, one of the country's most well regarded doctors, made this excellent argument against the lockdown

Source: https://www.post-gazette.com/opinion/Op-Ed/2020/05/14/Cyril-H-Wecht-Time-to-end-the-COVID-19-hysteria/stories/202005140031

Dr. Jayanta Bhattacharya is a professor of medicine at Stanford University. He said that people are "mistaken" if they think the lockdown will make people safe from COVID-19.

Source:
https://www.theblaze.com/news/stanford
-university-doctor-mistaken-coronavirus-
lockdowns

The Federalist wrote:

"Relapses are through the roof, overdoses are through the roof: How the pandemic is upping substance abuse"

"… They can't go to a 12-step based meeting…"

"… People are self-medicating due to the quarantine. And they're drinking more, and abusing more, and relapses are through the roof right now."

Source on the next page.

[https://thefederalist.com/2020/05/19/rela
pses-are-through-the-roof-overdoses-are-
through-the-roof-how-the-pandemic-is-
upping-substance-abuse/](https://thefederalist.com/2020/05/19/relapses-are-through-the-roof-overdoses-are-through-the-roof-how-the-pandemic-is-upping-substance-abuse/)

The Telegraph said that Neil Ferguson's Imperial model "could go down in history as the most devastating software mistake of all time, in terms of economic costs and lives lost."

Source:
[https://www.telegraph.co.uk/technology/
2020/05/16/neil-fergusons-imperial-
model-could-devastating-software-
mistake/](https://www.telegraph.co.uk/technology/2020/05/16/neil-fergusons-imperial-model-could-devastating-software-mistake/)

The Washongton Post wrote:

"Rise in female genital mutilation in Somalia linked to coronavirus shutdown"

"Somali girls out of school and stuck at

home have been subject to a 'massive rise' in female genital mutilation…"

"[Sadia Allin, Plan International's head of mission in Somalia, said] 'It's a lifetime torture for girls. The pain continues … until the girl goes to the grave. It impacts her education, ambition … everything.'"

"… the UNFPA has warned that globally 2 million more girls could be cut over the next decade because of how the global pandemic has disrupted efforts to end the practice."

Source: https://web.archive.org/web/20200519232914/https://www.washingtonpost.com/nation/2020/05/19/coronavirus-update-us/

More than 500 doctors signed this letter, which is says, "In medical terms, the shutdown was a mass casualty incident."

Source:
https://www.scribd.com/document/46231
9362/A-Doctor-a-Day-Letter-
Signed#fullscreen&from_embed

Dr. Mike deBoisblanc, head of the trauma department at John Muir Medical Center in Walnut Creek, California, said, "… we've seen a year's worth of suicide attempts in the last four weeks…"

Source: https://abc7news.com/suicide-covid-19-coronavirus-rates-during-pandemic-death-by/6201962/

Rampant unemployment, isolation and an uncertain future – could lead to 75,000 deaths from drug or alcohol abuse and suicide

Source:
https://www.cbsnews.com/news/coronav irus-deaths-suicides-drugs-alcohol-pandemic-75000/

In the U.S., the first nine weeks of the lockdown caused 38 million people to lose their jobs.

Source: https://thefederalist.com/2020/05/21/another-2-4-million-americans-filed-for-unemployment-last-week-38-million-since-march/

Neeraj Sood, a professor of health policy at the University of Southern California, said the fatality rate of COVID-19 "would probably be 0.13 percent for people outside nursing homes"

Source:

https://web.archive.org/web/20200603191311/https://www.washingtonpost.com/health/tell-me-what-to-do-please-even-experts-struggle-with-coronavirus-unknowns/2020/05/25/e11f9870-9d08-11ea-ad09-8da7ec214672_story.html

A scientific study of COVID-19 infection said, "Home outbreaks were the dominant category (254 of 318 outbreaks; 79.9%)"

Source: https://www.medrxiv.org/content/10.1101/2020.04.04.20053058v1.full.pdf

The New England Journal of Medicine wrote, "We know that wearing a mask outside health care facilities offers little, if any, protection from infection"

Source: https://www.nejm.org/doi/full/10.1056/NEJMp2006372

Knut Wittkowski, former head of Biostatistics, Epidemiology, and Research Design at The Rockefeller University's Center for Clinical and Translational Science, said the lockdown "most likely made the situation worse."

Source: https://www.spiked-online.com/2020/05/15/we-could-open-up-again-and-forget-the-whole-thing/

Denmark and Finland said they saw no increase in coronavirus infection rates after their schools re-opened.

Source: https://justthenews.com/world/europe/denmark-finland-say-they-saw-no-increase-coronavirus-after-schools-re-opened

Kanchan Soni, who lived in India, died because the lockdown prevented her from getting dialysis.

Source: https://www.newindianexpress.com/cities/delhi/2020/apr/16/dialysis-patient-denied-treatment-dies-2130804.html

Chewing gum, wire-cutters, and superglue: the alarming rise of DIY Dentistry under coronavirus

Source:
https://www.telegraph.co.uk/health-fitness/body/chewing-gum-wire-cutters-superglue-alarming-rise-diy-dentistry/

A scientific paper on the lockdown states, "In high burden settings, HIV, TB and malaria related deaths over 5 years may be increased by up to 10%, 20% and 36%, respectively."

Source:
https://www.imperial.ac.uk/media/imperial-college/medicine/mrc-gida/2020-05-01-COVID19-Report-19.pdf

The New York Times wrote:

"Polio and measles could surge after disruption of vaccine programs. A new study of 129 countries found that the interruption of inoculation efforts could put 80 million babies at risk of getting deadly, preventable diseases."

Source:
https://www.nytimes.com/2020/05/22/health/coronavirus-polio-measles-immunizations.html

The World Health Organization said, "If you are healthy, you only need to wear a mask if you are taking care of a person with COVID-19."

Source:
https://abcnews.go.com/Health/cdc-offer-conflicting-advice-masks-expert-tells-us/story?id=70958380

Reopening schools in Denmark did not worsen outbreak, data shows.

Source: https://www.reuters.com/article/us-health-coronavirus-denmark-reopening-idUSKBN2341N7

One month later: top Israeli mathematician predicted COVID-19 peaks after 40 days with or without economic lockdowns – and he was right!

Source: https://www.thegatewaypundit.com/2020/05/one-month-later-top-israeli-mathematician-predicted-covid-19-peaks-40-days-without-economic-lockdowns-right/

Dr. Kelly Fradin said, "I'm a pediatrician and I think we should reopen schools, even with the risk of coronavirus outbreaks."

Source: https://www.insider.com/pediatrician-reopen-schools-even-if-it-leads-coronavirus-outbreaks-2020-6

This video is from June 2020. It shows Dr. Anthony Fauci removing his mask right after the TV cameras stop filming.

https://www.bitchute.com/video/5lQDVpDybb58/

The New York Times wrote:

"Slowing the coronavirus is speeding the spread of other diseases. Many mass immunization efforts worldwide were halted this spring to prevent spread of the virus at crowded inoculation sites.

The consequences have been alarming…"

"... cargo flights with vaccine supplies were halted…"

"Now, diphtheria is appearing in Pakistan, Bangladesh and Nepal. Cholera is in South Sudan, Cameroon, Mozambique, Yemen and Bangladesh. A mutated strain of poliovirus has been reported in more than 30 countries. And measles is flaring around the globe, including in Bangladesh, Brazil, Cambodia, Central African Republic, Iraq, Kazakhstan, Nepal, Nigeria and Uzbekistan."

Source:
https://www.nytimes.com/2020/06/14/health/coronavirus-vaccines-measles.html

Norway health chief: lockdown was not needed to tame Covid

Source:
https://www.spectator.co.uk/article/norway-health-chief-lockdown-was-not-needed-to-tame-covid

NPR wrote:

"Antibody tests point to lower death rate for the coronavirus than first thought."

"Mounting evidence suggests the coronavirus is more common and less deadly than it first appeared."

Source:
https://www.npr.org/sections/health-shots/2020/05/28/863944333/antibody-tests-point-to-lower-death-rate-for-the-coronavirus-than-first-thought

Coronavirus pandemic could push 122 million to brink of starvation: Oxfam

Source: https://globalnews.ca/news/7155931/coronavirus-starvation-oxfam/

Dr. Dan Wohlgelernter said:

"What we needed to do was not lock down all of society. Not shut down schools. Not shut down all businesses. You needed to protect the elderly. Particularly the elderly in the nursing homes. It's a small segment of our population. We could have allowed the rest of the population to continue with their lives, take adequate precautions but not be completely shut down. The cost of the shut down in terms of the physical, emotional, and psychological health of people is enormous. We've only seen the tip of the iceberg of people who have been shut-in. Who've lost their businesses. Who are facing depression. Who are facing issues of mental health because of the consequences. This should never happen again. If we ever face this situation again we need to learn the lessons from the mistakes and policies that were implemented."

Source:
https://theohiostar.com/2020/07/01/doctors-break-down-covid-response-and-the-demonization-of-hcq-doctors-tell-all/

People are more likely to contract COVID-19 at home, study finds

Source:
https://www.yahoo.com/news/people-more-likely-contract-covid-122611396.html

The Times wrote:

"No known case of teacher catching coronavirus from pupils, says scientist. There has been no recorded case of a teacher catching the coronavirus from a pupil anywhere in the world, according to one of the government's leading scientific advisers. Mark Woolhouse, a leading epidemiologist and member of the government's Sage committee, told The Times that it may have been a mistake to close schools in March given the limited role children play in spreading the virus."

Source:
https://www.thetimes.co.uk/article/no-known-case-of-teacher-catching-coronavirus-from-pupils-says-scientist-3zk5g2x6z

Coronavirus lockdown 'made no difference to number of deaths', study claims.

Source: https://www.the-sun.com/news/1190721/coronavirus-lockdown-no-difference/

Citing educational risks, scientific panel urges that schools reopen.

Source: https://www.nytimes.com/2020/07/15/health/coronavirus-schools-reopening.html

Stanford doctor Scott Atlas says the science shows kids should go back to school.

Source: https://thefederalist.com/2020/07/15/stanford-doctor-scott-atlas-says-the-science-shows-kids-should-go-back-to-school/

German study finds no evidence coronavirus spreads in schools.

Source:
https://www.telegraph.co.uk/news/2020/07/13/german-study-finds-no-evidence-coronavirus-spreads-schools/

As of September 2020, Sweden, which never had a lockdown, or a mask mandate, had a lower total, cumulative per capita COVID-19 death rate than the U.S.

Sources:
https://web.archive.org/web/20200907000001/https://www.worldometers.info/coronavirus/

https://reason.com/2020/09/11/the-covid-19-death-toll-is-rising-much-faster-in-the-u-s-than-in-sweden-which-now-has-fewer-deaths-per-capita/

John Tierney, a contributing science columnist for the New York Times, wrote:

"The chief effect of school closures is to hurt students. In St. Paul, Minnesota, where schools have been mostly closed since March, 40 percent of the students are failing this quarter—double the normal rate. In the Dallas public schools, which closed in March and reopened late this fall, recent tests revealed that half of the students have regressed in mathematics since last year, and that's probably typical of the 'learning loss' that will have long-lasting effects on students around the world. Economists at the World Bank estimate that the spring closures will ultimately reduce the affected students' lifetime earnings by 5 percent - a loss totaling $10 trillion worldwide. Extrapolating from the well-established effects of education and income on life expectancy, another team of researchers calculates that the springtime school closures in the United States will shorten students' lives by a cumulative total of more than five million years - more years of life than were lost to the pandemic in the spring."

Source: https://www.city-journal.org/bidens-covid-advisors-ignore-high-costs-of-lockdowns

Jay Bhattacharya, Stanford doctor, calls lockdowns the "biggest public health mistake we've ever made"

Source on next page.

https://www.newsweek.com/stanford-doctor-calls-lockdowns-biggest-public-health-mistake-weve-ever-made-1574540

Doctors indicate startling rise in child suicide, psychiatric admissions from lockdown.

Source: https://elizabethjohnston.org/doctors-indicate-startling-rise-in-child-suicide-psychiatric-admissions-amid-ongoing-pandemic-measures

The lockdown made it harder for victims of domestic violence to seek help.

Source: https://www.city-journal.org/lockdowns-and-domestic-violence

Pew Research: Lockdowns prompting devastating levels of 'psychological distress' among young people.

Source: https://fee.org/articles/pew-research-survey-lockdowns-prompting-devastating-levels-of-psychological-distress-among-young-people/

There's no proof that lockdowns save lives, but plenty of evidence that they end them.

Source: https://www.city-journal.org/death-and-lockdowns

A scientific paper states:

"We estimate the size of the COVID-19-relatedunemployment shock to be between 2 and 5 times larger than the typical unemployment shock, depending on race and gender, resulting in a significant increase in mortality rates and drop in life expectancy. We also predict that the shock will disproportionately affect African-Americans and women, over a short horizon, while the effects for white men will unfold over longer horizons. These figures translate in more than 0.8 million additional deaths over the next 15 years."

Source:
https://www.nber.org/system/files/working_papers/w28304/w28304.pdf

Lockdowns do not control the Coronavirus: The evidence

Source:
https://www.aier.org/article/lockdowns-do-not-control-the-coronavirus-the-evidence/

The data shows lockdowns end more lives than they save.

Source: https://nypost.com/2021/03/22/the-data-shows-lockdowns-end-more-lives-than-they-save/

Child suicides are rising during lockdown.

Source: https://medicalxpress.com/news/2021-02-child-suicides-lockdown.html

Escalating suicide rates among school children during COVID-19 pandemic and lockdown period: An alarming psychosocial issue.

Source: https://journals.sagepub.com/doi/full/10.1177/0253717620982514

Child suicides rising during lockdown.

Source:
https://www.webmd.com/lung/news/20210210/child-suicides-rising-during-lockdown

Suicide among children during Covid-19 pandemic: An alarming social issue

Source:
https://www.ncbi.nlm.nih.gov/pmc/articles/PMC7500342/

Surge of student suicides pushes Las Vegas schools to reopen.

Source:
https://web.archive.org/web/20210201004833/https://www.nytimes.com/2021/01/24/us/politics/student-suicides-nevada-coronavirus.html

Global rise in childhood mental health issues amid lockdown.

Source:
https://abcnews.go.com/Lifestyle/wireStory/amid-pandemic-international-epidemic-childhood-pain-76409892